Caruso's Caricatures

ENRICO CARUSO

Dover Publications, Inc.
New York

Published in Canada by General Publishing Company, Ltd.,
30 Lesmill Road, Don Mills, Toronto, Ontario.
Published in the United Kingdom by Constable and Company, Ltd., 10 Orange Street, London WC2H 7EG.

Caruso's Caricatures, first published by Dover Publications,
Inc., in 1977, is a new selection of pictures from three editions (1922, 1939, 1965) of *Caricatures by Enrico Caruso*,
published by *La Follia di New York*, New York. In the present
volume the picture arrangement, captions and other text
matter have been extensively revised, and several hitherto
unpublished pictures have been added. The present edition
is published by special arrangement with Mr. Michael Sisca
of *La Follia di New York* and Dr. Francis Sisca.

International Standard Book Number: 0-486-23528-9
Library of Congress Catalog Card Number 77-77704

Manufactured in the United States of America
Dover Publications, Inc.
180 Varick Street
New York, N.Y. 10014

CONTENTS

The Caricatures

HOW I DISCOVERED
THE CARICATURIST CARUSO
by Marziale Sisca

On the evening of November 23, 1903, when Enrico Caruso made his first appearance in *Rigoletto* at the Metropolitan Opera House, I was present at the performance. Caruso took the audience by storm. The next morning, I wrote him a card of congratulation and admiration, and asked him to send me a photograph to be published in *La Follia,* the newspaper of the New York Italian community I had begun to publish ten years earlier. Caruso replied with a kind letter of thanks, but expressed his regret that he could not send me a photograph because— he did not have one! However, he sent a sketch which I inserted in the next issue of *La Follia* (at that time a weekly). In this sketch I noticed something that attracted my attention: the clear signs of the multiformity of the artist's genius. I began to pay visits to Caruso, and soon our relationship was cemented into the most fraternal friendship.

At that time, the caricatural sketches for *La Follia* were done by the late Peppino Stella, a very strong colorist who left indelible traces on the American pictorial school. An annual event in the Italian colony was the banquet of the Italian Chamber of Commerce. For the special work of covering this event, Peppino Stella requested an extra fee of twenty dollars, and I submitted willy-nilly. Next day, Stella demanded that I should supply him with the evening dress as well. Since he refused to go to one of the numerous rental houses and insisted that I buy him a new one, I had to give up the idea of entrusting him with the task.

I had a bold inspiration: I thought at once of Caruso. Going to the Plaza Hotel where he was staying, I timidly made the request with little hope of favorable response. I could scarcely believe my ears when he accepted the stint without reluctance.

The following Saturday the ballroom of the Astor was filled to capacity. Caruso sat at the table of honor. During the evening the now famous Caruso, while smiling and joking with admirers, worked feverishly to caricature the guests.

The account of the banquet appeared in *La Follia,* studded with numerous excellent vignettes. The weekly was rapidly sold out. From that day, Caruso became the permanent caricaturist of *La Follia.* Every issue published his sketches which, sure enough, were the most irresistible attraction. Circulation rose, winning readers even among those who did not know Italian.

One day the elder Joseph Pulitzer sent one of his editors to Caruso, offering him fifty thousand dollars a year for one new cartoon each week to be published in the *World.* Caruso thanked him but refused the offer. "But how much does Sisca pay you?" "He does not pay anything, but for my sketches I have already chosen the paper that most attracted me, and you know that we Italians have a wise and simple proverb which teaches that 'where there is pleasure there is no loss.'"

For nearly eighteen consecutive years *La Follia* published thousands of caricatures by the immortal singer. During his memorable seasons at the Metropolitan, Caruso personally delivered his drawings to his "carissimo Marziale." When he went on tour, he never forgot to send his sketches by special delivery to "his favorite newspaper."

After official receptions, grand banquets with sovereigns, statesmen, generals, admirals, leaders and personalities of the international world, the genial caricaturist caught the most characteristic features of his subjects and mailed the sketches at once to *La Follia.* Admirers preserved them zealously in prized collections.

By now, Caruso was not only idolized as a singer with an angelic voice, but was greatly admired for his caricatures as well. Unlike most professional caricaturists who cannot rid themselves of their passions and biases and use their art as a formidable weapon, Caruso made use of his sketches as an inspiring pastime to arouse hilarity and good humor. Caricature for him was an aristocratic and kindly art through which he enjoyed exhibiting his friends and the colleagues and personalities he most admired or who stirred his creative resourcefulness.

For this reason his work gushed spontaneously from his remarkable imagination.

Caruso's contributions to *La Follia* ceased only with the end of his life in 1921. His last vignette [No. 364 in the present volume] was mailed from Sorrento sixteen days before he died. On July 29, four days before his death, he sent a warm and friendly letter in which he gave me news of his illness and closed with these words:

"My voice, however, has nothing to do with my illness. In fact, a few days ago, to the surprise of all, I sang the aria from *Martha* and the Bastianellis [his doctors] assured me that in four or five months I will be able to resume my work. I sent you a caricature of the famous Sicilian actor Giovanni Grasso, who will come to America this fall. I hope you have received it. No more at present. We all send our best regards to you and your family. Cordially yours, Enrico."

Who could have foreseen that the aria from *Martha* would be his swan song, and the sketch of Grasso the last caricature drawn by his skillful hand?

PREFACE
TO THE DOVER EDITION
by Michael Sisca

The genius of Caruso was twofold: as singer and as caricaturist. It is not the premise of this volume to review his incomparable voice—one the like of which will never be heard again—but rather the Caruso genius in another avenue, that of graphics. Recalling that these two gifts were contained in one man, one can truly repeat the adjective "incomparable."

The hundreds of caricatures drawn for *La Follia*, which was then published by my father, were regarded by Caruso as the newspaper's exclusive property. Because of their love and affection for each other, my father never exploited Caruso's drawing talent in worldwide fashion, that is, outside *La Follia* (though a collection of the caricatures in book form with the *La Follia* imprint went through several editions). The time has come, over 55 years after the tenor's death, for the world to be reminded of his extraordinary creative talent as a draftsman. Now that I am editor and publisher of the monthly *La Follia di New York*, and have inherited the entire collection of caricatures in my father's possession, I have arranged with Dover Publications to make this edition available to all who remember the great singer.

I felt the surging interest in Caruso when, in 1973, I was invited to Oslo by Norwegian television to do a one-hour program on the occasion of the hundredth anniversary of his birth. The honor and enthusiasm accorded were tremendous.

The first opera I attended at the Metropolitan was *The Girl of the Golden West* with Caruso, Amato, Destinn, Didur, de Segurola and Gilly in the cast, and Toscanini conducting. A few days later my father invited Caruso, Amato and Puccini to dinner. Casually, Caruso began to sketch Puccini (who, by the way, had a prominent nose). I asked Caruso, "How do you sketch?" He answered, "Per me è molto facile [for me it's very easy]—the only thing you have to do is pick out the most pronounced feature on the face and work around that feature. E hai trovato la caricatura [and you have found your caricature]."

Self-Portraits

1

2

3

4

5

6

8

7

9

10

11

14 & 15: The faces are entirely made up of numerals.

17

16

21

22

23

22: This is a topsy-turvy picture; upside down, it represents Kaiser Wilhelm.
23: Caruso's last self-portrait.

Other Opera Singers

24: Caruso and Geraldine Farrar at a rehearsal.

25. Feodor Chaliapin.

26: Milka Ternina. 27: Pol Plançon and a follower. 28: María Barrientos.

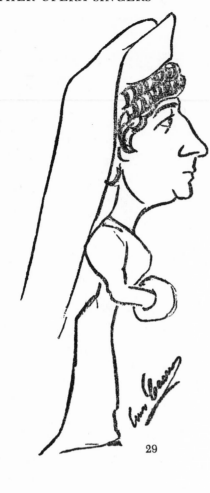

29

30

31

29: Johanna Gadski. 30: Victor Maurel. 31: John McCormack.

32: Emmy Destinn. 33: Luisa Tetrazzini.

34: Beniamino Gigli. 35: Geraldine Farrar. 36: Nellie Melba.

37: Adamo Didur. 38: Leo Slezak.

39–42: Antonio Scotti.

43–46: Antonio Scotti.

47: Lucrezia Bori.

48: Marcella Sembrich. 49 & 50: Giuseppe de Luca.

51: (Probably) Lillian Nordica. 52: Nordica and her voice teacher Simonson.
53: Antonio Scotti and Louise Homer at a rehearsal conducted by Arturo Vigna.

54: Louise Homer. 55: Giovanni Zenatello.

56: Amelita Galli-Curci. 57: Marcel Journet. 58: Jean de Reszke.

59: Eugenio Giraldoni. 60: Helen Mapleson.

61: Lydia Lipkowska. 62: Bessie Abott.

63: Luisa Villani. 64: Francesco Daddi. 65: Aristodemo Giorgini. 66: Giovanni Martino.

67: Hermann Weil. 68: Nina Morgana. 69: Goettlich (Hans Göttich?). 70: Armand LeComte (reproduced from original drawing).

71: Otto Goritz. 72: Mario Sammarco. 73: Franz Naval.

74: Eduardo Missiano, Caruso's discoverer (reproduced from original drawing).
75: Taurino Parvis. 76: Giulio Rossi. 77: Lina Cavalieri.

78: Robert Blass. 79: Luca Botta. 80: Riccardo Stracciari. 81: Vittorio Arimondi.

82: María Gay. 83 & 84: Tullio Voghera (also a conductor).

85: Pompilio Malatesta. 86: Fernando Carpi. 87: M. Baillard.

88: Walter Soomer. 89: Bernard Bégué. 90: Andrea (Andrés) de Segurola.
91: Gabriella Besanzoni.

92: First full rehearsal of *La Fanciulla del West* ("gruppo coristi" = a group of chorus members).

Singers in Operatic Roles

93: Caruso as Count Maurizio. 94: Lina Cavalieri as Adriana.

95: Caruso as Radames.

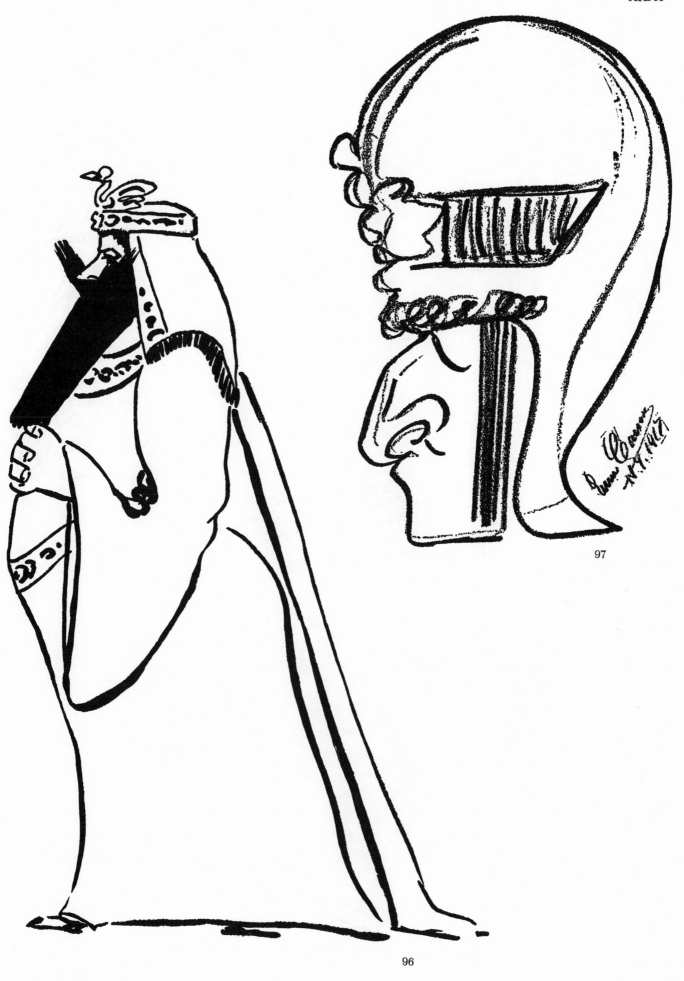

97

96

96: Pol Plançon as Ramfis. 97: Giovanni Martinelli as Radames.

98: Antonio Scotti as Amonasro. 99: Caruso as Radames. 100: Pasquale Amato as Amonasro.

101: Emmy Destinn as Aïda. 102: Adamo Didur as Ramfis. 103: Emma Eames as Aïda.

104: Amedeo Bassi as Andrea Chenier. 105: Caruso as Renaud.

106 & 107: Caruso as Count Riccardo.

108

109

108: Andrea de Segurola as Samuel. 109: Andreas Dippel as Count Almaviva.

110: Alessandro Bonci as Almaviva and Feodor Chaliapin as Don Basilio. 111: Bonci as Almaviva.

112: Caruso as Rodolfo. 113: Adamo Didur as Schaunard. 114: Andrea de Segurola as Colline.

115: Caruso as Rodolfo. 116: Benoit, the landlord. 117: Antonio Pini-Corsi as Benoit.
118: Giuseppe Campanari as Marcello.

119: Antonio Scotti as Marcello. 120: Marcella Sembrich as Mimi. 121: Caruso as Rodolfo. 122: Gina Viafora as Mimi.

123 & 124: Caruso as Don José. 125: Emma Calvé as Carmen.

126: Caruso as Turiddu.

127

127: Celestina Boninsegna as Santuzza.

128

128: Antonio Scotti as Crispino.

129: Pasquale Amato as Cyrano (no doubt inspired by the Cubists in the Armory Show
of 1913).

130

131

132

133

130: Andrea de Segurola as Arlecchino. 131: Angelo Bada as Leandro. 132: Antonio Scotti as Lelio. 133: Antonio Pini-Corsi as Pantalone.

134

135

136

137

134: Giulio Rossi as Menego. 135: Hermann Jadlowker as Florindo. 136: Adamo Didur as Ottavio. 137: Jeanne Maubourg as Beatrice.

138

139

138: Antonio Scotti as Malatesta, Andreas Dippel as Ernesto, Bernard Bégué as the Notary, Marcella Sembrich as Norina, and Archangelo Rossi as Don Pasquale. 139: Caruso as Nemorino.

140

141

140: Antonio Scotti as Belcore. 141: Caruso as Nemorino.

142: Antonio Scotti as Falstaff. 143: Jacques Bars as Gaspar. 144: Antonio Scotti as Alfonso.

145: Caruso as Fernando. 146: Andrea de Segurola as the minstrel Jake Wallace.
147: Pasquale Amato as the sheriff Jack Rance.

148: Adamo Didur as Ashby. 149: Caruso as Dick Johnson.

150: Giulio Rossi as Sid. 151: Dinh Gilly as Sonora. 152: Emmy Destinn as Minnie.

153

154

153: Caruso as Dick Johnson. 154: Pol Plançon as Mephistopheles.

155: Antonio Scotti as Valentin. 156: Caruso as Faust. 157: Josephine Jacoby as Siebel.

GRISOGONO (PINI-CORSI)

158 & 159: Caruso as Don Alvaro (158 is signed "Dorothy Caruso"). 160: Giuseppe de Luca as Don Carlo. 161: Antonio Pini-Corsi as Crisogono.

162

163

162: Adamo Didur as Pastor Stapps. 163: Pasquale Amato as Carlo Worms.

FEDERICO
(CARUSO)

PALM
(ROSSI)

164

165

164: Caruso as Federico Loewe. 165: Giulio Rossi as Giovanni Palm.

166: Eduardo Missiano as Chief of Police. 167: Caruso as Enzo. 168: Otto Goritz as the broom-maker Peter.

169: Antonio Scotti as Kyoto. 170: Caruso as Osaka. 171: Emma Eames as Iris.

172

173

174

175

172: Léon Rothier as Cardinal Brogni. 173: Giuseppe Bonfiglio, leading dancer in the ballet sequence. 174: Caruso as Eleazar. 175: Orville Harrold as Leopold.

176

177

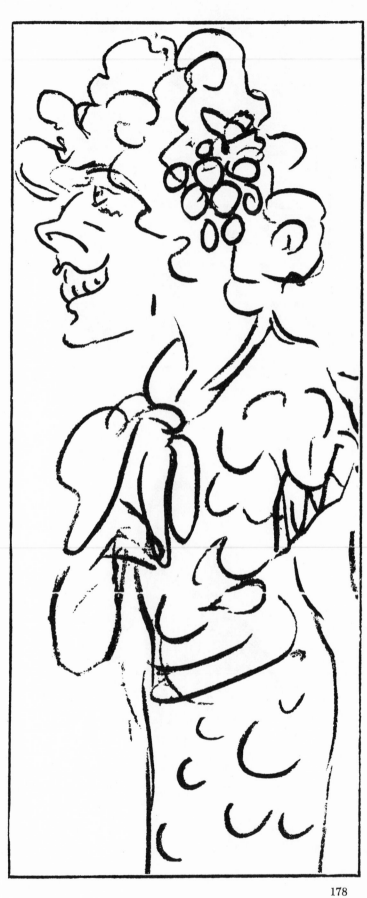

178

176: Rosa Ponselle as Rachel. 177: A page. 178: Geraldine Farrar as Louise.

179: Dinh Gilly as the High Priest. 180: Caruso as Julien.

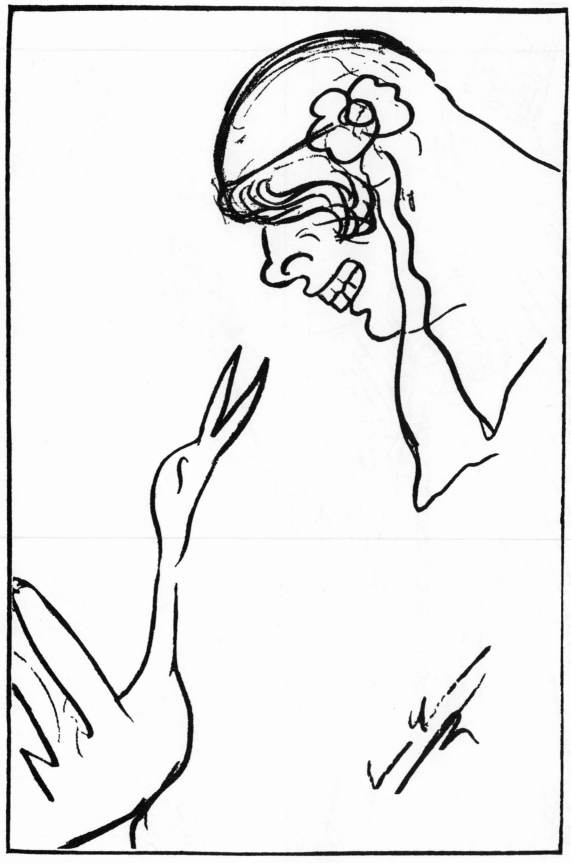

181

181: Geraldine Farrar as the Goose Girl.

182: Otto Goritz as the Fiddler. 183: Hermann Jadlowker as the King's Son.

184

185

186

184: Adamo Didur as Antonio. 185: Caruso as Flammen. 186: Geraldine Farrar as Lodoletta.

187

189

188

187: Andrea de Segurola as Franz. 188: Pasquale Amato as Gianetto. 189: Gustavo Berl-Resky as Ashton.

190

190: Luca Botta as Pinkerton (reproduced from original drawing).

191: Caruso as Pinkerton, Antonio Scotti as Sharpless, Angelo Bada as Goro, and Geraldine Farrar as Cio-Cio-San.

192: Geraldine Farrar as Cio-Cio-San. 193: Giovanni Martinelli as Lefebvre.
194: Geraldine Farrar as Caterina Hübscher.

195: Pasquale Amato as Napoleon. 196: Antonio Scotti as Lescaut. 197: Andrea de Segurola as Geronte.

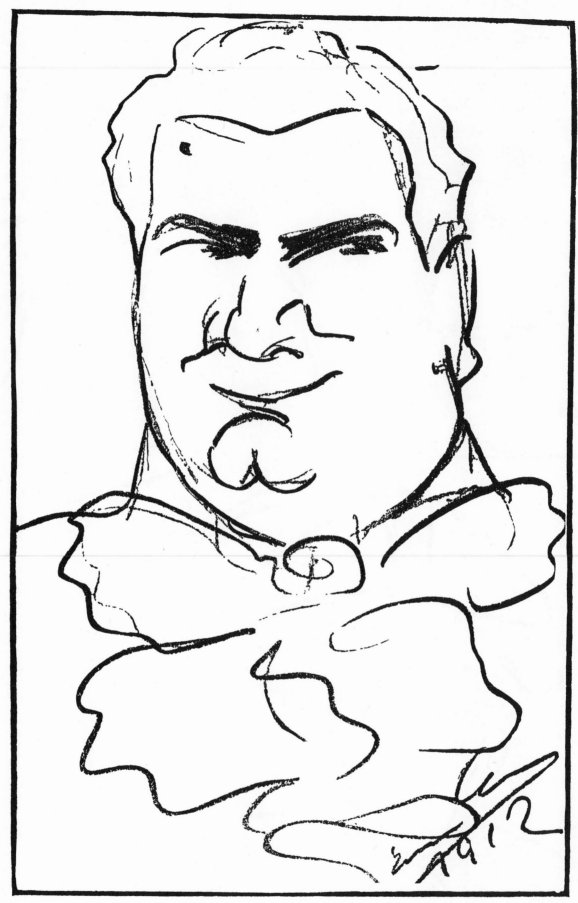

198

198: Caruso as Des Grieux.

199: Caruso as Lionel. 200: Giuseppe de Luca as Plunkett. 201: María Barrientos as
Lady Harriet.

202: Feodor Chaliapin as Mefistofele. 203: Johannes Sembach as Walther von Stolzing.
204: Otto Goritz as Beckmesser.

205: Antonio Scotti as Chim-Fen. 206: Lucrezia Bori as Ah-Yoe.

207

207: Caruso as Canio.

208

209

210

208: Mario Sammarco as Tonio. 209: Armand Crabbé as Silvio. 210: Olive Fremstad as Kundry.

211:Frieda Hempel as Leila. 212: Caruso as Nadir. 213: Giuseppe de Luca as Zurga.
214: Léon Rothier as Nourabad.

215: Caruso as John of Leyden. 216: Carl Burrian (Karel Burian) as Herod. 217 &
218: Other characters. 219: The final moment.

220: Bianca Froelich, who performed the Dance of the Seven Veils. 221–224: Olive
Fremstad as Salome. 225: Marion Weed as Herodias.

226: A soldier. 227: Weed as Herodias. 228: Another character. 229: Burrian as Herod.
230: Anton Van Rooy as Jokanaan. 231: A soldier.

232

232: Caruso as Samson.

233 & 234: Caruso as Samson.

235: Mathilde Bauermeister as Teresa. 236: Bernard Bégué as Alessio. 237: Pol Plançon as Rodolfo.

238 & 239: Antonio Scotti as Scarpia. 240 & 241: Other characters.

243

242

244

242: Anton Van Rooy as Kurwenal. 243: Robert Blass, probably as Hunding in *Die Walküre*. 244: Florence Mulford as Grimgerde.

245
246

245: Riccardo Martin as Giuseppe Hagenbach. 246: Pasquale Amato as Vincenzo
Gellner.

247

247: Bella Alten as Papagena and Otto Goritz as Papageno.

248

248: Geraldine Farrar as Zaza.

249: Minnie Egener as Natalia. 250: Pasquale Amato as Cascart.

251

252

251. Giulio Crimi as Milio Dufresne. 252: Otto Goritz as Zsupan.

Conductors

253

253: Arturo Toscanini.

254 & 255: Arturo Toscanini.

256 & 257: Arturo Toscanini.

259

258

260

258 & 259: Gennaro Papi. 260: The chorus master Nepoti (perhaps the tenor Lodovico
Nepoti, who sang in the Met premiere of *Germania* in 1910).

261

On board S.S. "Canopic"

262

261: Cleofonte Campanini. 262: Arnaldo Conti.

263

263: Alfred Hertz.

264–267: Alfred Hertz.

268: Giuseppe Bamboschek.

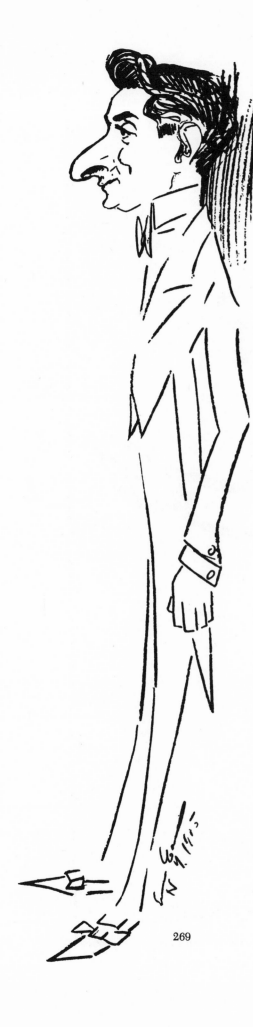

269

270

269: Gaetano Bavagnoli. 270: Vincenzo Bellezza.

271

271: Francesco Spetrino.

272

273

274

275

276

277

272–277: Arturo Vigna.

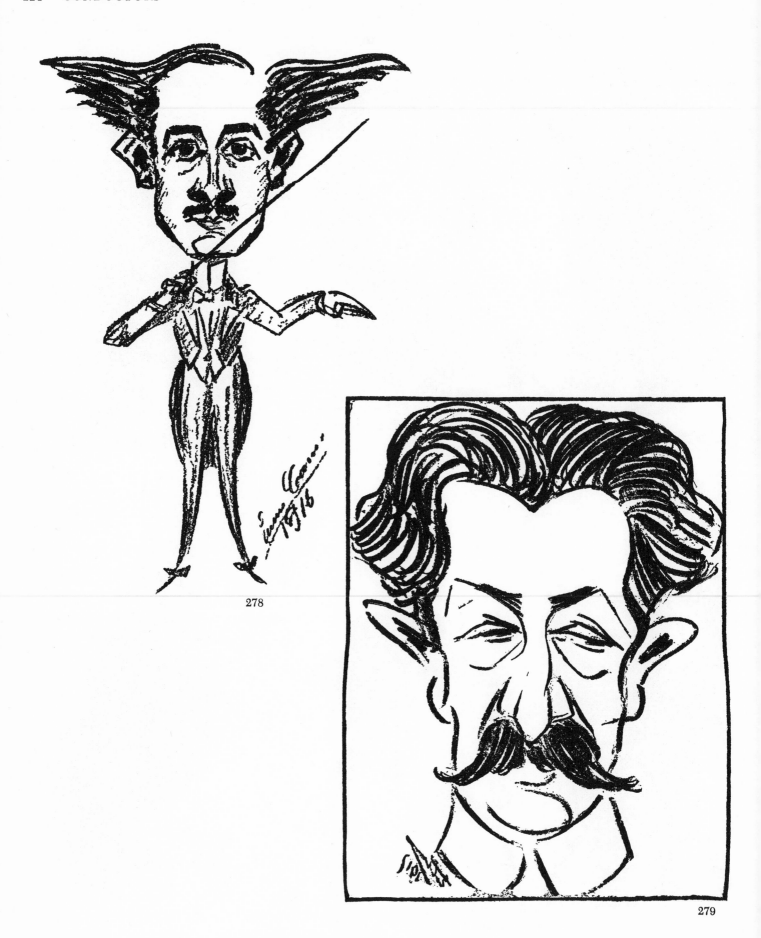

278: Giorgio Polacco. 279: Pierre Monteux.

280: Giulio Setti. 281: Egisto Tango.

282: Oscar Anselmi. 283: Hans Morgenstern. 284: Kurt Schindler and Paul Eissler.

285: Nahan Franko. 286: Rodolfo Ferrari.

287

287: Vittorio Podesti.

Composers

288: Gioacchino Rossini.

289

289: Giuseppe Verdi.

290

290: Giuseppe Verdi.

291: Richard Strauss. 292: Gustave Charpentier.

293: Friedrich von Flotow. 294: Vincenzo Bellini.

295 & 296: Giacomo Puccini (in 295, he holds a *Fanciulla del West* figure).

298

297

297 & 298: Giacomo Puccini.

299: Arrigo Boito. 300: Ruggiero Leoncavallo. 301: Pietro Mascagni.

303

302

302: Camille Saint-Saëns. 303: Jules Massenet.

304: Francesco Cilèa. 305: Engelbert Humperdinck.

306

307

306: Ermanno Wolf-Ferrari. 307: Arturo Buzzi-Peccia.

308

308: Gustav Mahler (also a conductor).

309: Giuseppe (Gino) Marinuzzi (also a conductor). 310: Richard Barthélemy.

311

311: Umberto Giordano.

312

313

312: Ernesto De Curtis. 313: Caruso with Giordano.

314: Victor Herbert (also a conductor). 315: Riccardo Zandonai.

316

316: Enrique Granados.

317 & 318: Francesco Paolo Tosti.

319

319: Mario Costa.

Instrumentalists

320: Pier Adolfo Tirindelli, violinist (also a composer).

321

322

321 & 322: Mischa Elman, violinist.

323: Mischa Elman. 324: Harold Bauer, pianist.

325: Jessie Baskerville, pianist. 326: Fritz Kreisler, violinist.

327: Arrigo Serato, violinist. 328: Wilhelm Stengel, pianist (husband of Marcella Sembrich). 329: Paolo Martucci, pianist.

330: Josef Hofmann, pianist. 331: Maria Farruggio, violinist.

332: Vassily Safonov, pianist (also a conductor). 333: August Spanuth, pianist.

334: Studies of orchestra musicians.

334

Impresarios and Managers

335: Giulio Gatti-Casazza addressing Met singers (the two men at the left appear to be Caruso and Scotti).

336 & 337: Giulio Gatti-Casazza.

339

338

338 & 339: Giulio Gatti-Casazza.

340

342

341

340: Oscar Hammerstein. 341: Caruso's manager in Germany. 342: Andreas Dippel (also a singer).

343

343: Edward Ziegler.

344

345

344: Henry Russell. 345: Daniel Frohman.

346: Arthur Hammerstein. 347: Earl Carroll (in 1912, when this drawing was made,
chiefly a songwriter; theatrical manager from 1919).

348

348: Heinrich Conried.

349: David Belasco (also a playwright). 350: Jesse Lasky.

Dancers, Actors
and Entertainers

351: Anna Pavlova, ballerina.

352: Giuseppe Bonfiglio, dancer and ballet master at the Met. 353: Rosina Galli, dancer at the Met. 354: William Gillette, actor and playwright.

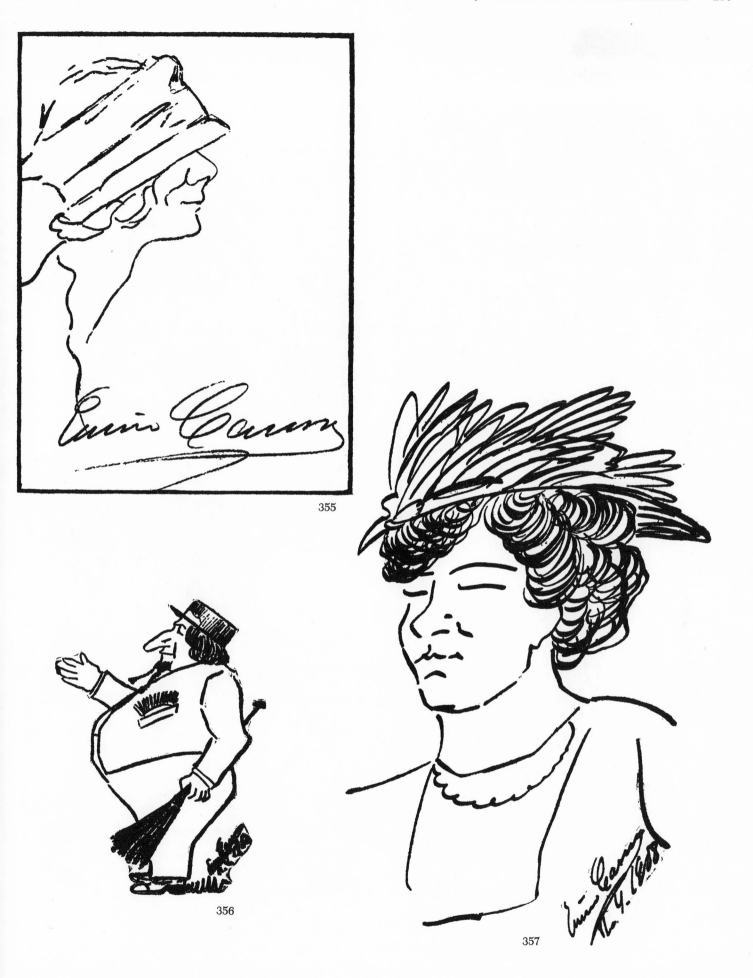

355: Ruth Donnelly, actress. 356: Joseph M. Weber (of Weber & Fields), comedian and manager. 357: Lillian Russell, singer and actress.

358

359

360

358 & 359: Ermete Novelli, Italian actor (in 358, as Othello). 360: Irene Bordoni, musical-comedy star.

361

361: Raymond Hitchcock, comedian.

362

363

362: Gaby Deslys, musical-comedy star. 363: Benoît-Constant Coquelin (*aîné*),
French actor.

364: Giovanni Grasso, Italian actor (this was Caruso's last caricature). 365: Yvette
Guilbert, French actress and diseuse. 366: Ethel Barrymore, actress.

367: Gertie Millar, London musical-comedy star. 368: Julia Marlowe, actress.

Transformations

369: Caruso Easter Egg No. 3, with Met conductor Giulio Setti and stage manager Romei.

370

371

372

373

374

370: Caruso. 371: Alfred Hertz, conductor (heart = Herz). 372: Alfred Selisberg.
373: Antonio Scotti, singer. 374: Luigi Roversi, journalist.

375

376

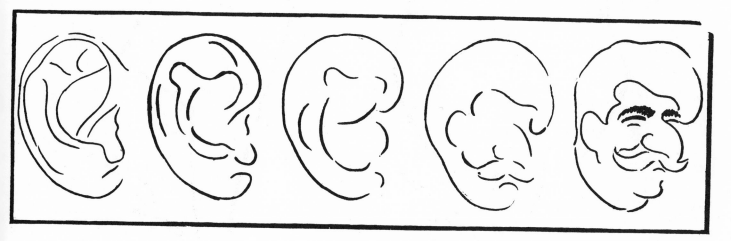

377

375: Arturo Toscanini, conductor. 376: Giacomo Puccini, composer. 377: Nahan Franko, conductor.

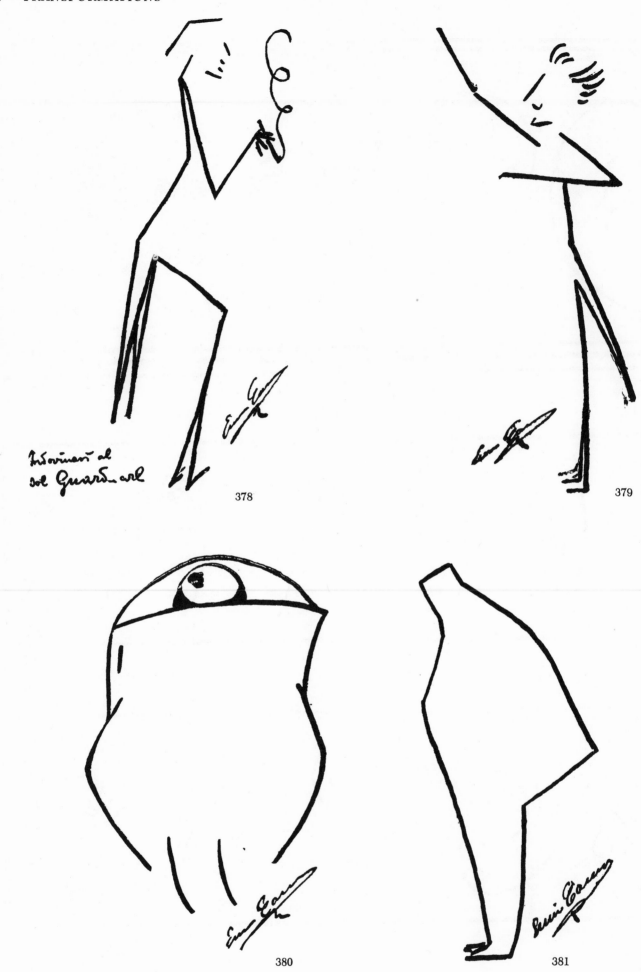

378: William J. Guard, press agent. 379: Toscanini. 380: Hertz. 381: Giulio Gatti-Casazza, impresario.

382: Caruso Easter Egg No. 2 (with many characters who appear elsewhere in this
volume).

383

383: Caruso Easter Egg No. 1 (self-portrait with good wishes to readers of *La Follia*).

Miscellaneous

384

384: Marcellino Caruso, the tenor's father.

385

386

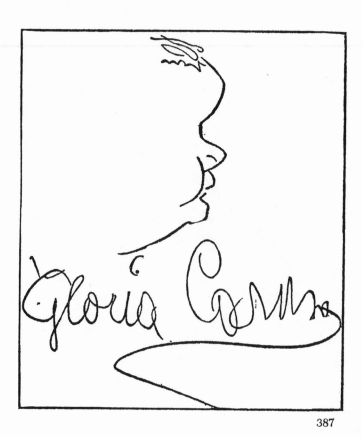

387

385: Giovanni Caruso, the tenor's brother. 386: Dorothy Benjamin Caruso, the tenor's second wife. 387: Their daughter Gloria.

388

389

388: Tito Ricordi, of the Milan music publishers. 389: Calvin G. Childs, recording
repertoire director of the Victor Talking Machine Co.

390

390: Caruso and the sons of his publisher at *La Follia,* Francis (now Dr. Francis)
Sisca and Michael (Osvaldo) Sisca, present publisher of the magazine.

391: Marziale Sisca, original publisher of Caruso's caricatures in *La Follia*.

392: Giovanni Porzio, lawyer, Caruso's executor. 393: Bruno Zirato, Caruso's secretary.

394: Dr. P. M. Marafioti, physician and voice teacher. 395: Simonson, voice teacher
of Lillian Nordica. 396: William Thorner, voice teacher.

397: Jules Speck, a Met stage manager (reproduced from original drawing).

398: Jules Speck. 399: William J. Guard, the Met's press agent.

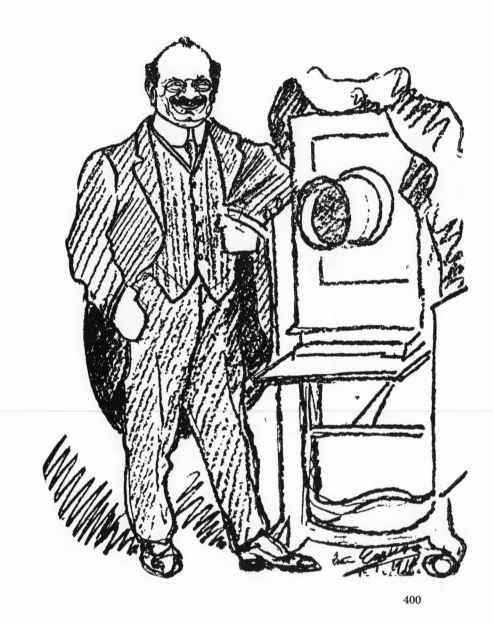

400

400: Herman Mishkin, official Met photographer.

401: Mario Marchese, Met prompter. 402: Florence Morton, Met telephone operator.

403: Marco Praga, writer. 404: Pierre Wolff, French playwright (reproduced from original drawing).

405: Gaston de Caillavet, French playwright (reproduced from original drawing).
406: Luigi Barzini (the elder), journalist and writer (father of the author of *The Italians*).

407

407: Maurice Maeterlinck, Belgian playwright and author.

408: Giovanni Verga, Italian novelist and playwright. 409: Dr. Luigi Roversi, journalist.

410: Roberto Bracco, author of Neapolitan song texts. 411: Camillo Antona Traversi,
journalist.

MA CHÊRIE!

413

412

414

412: Pieretto Bianco, portrait painter. 413: Edmondo Pizzella, portrait painter.
414: Gaetano Scognamiglio, antique dealer.

415: Andrew Carnegie, steel magnate and philanthropist.

415

415: Andrew Carnegie, steel magnate and philanthropist.

416: Otto H. Kahn, banker, patron of the Met. 417: George Gould, railroad executive.

418

419

418: Romano Avezzana, Italian ambassador to the U.S. 419: Dr. Ettore Tresca, physician, brother of the famous socialist Carlo Tresca.

420: Charles Evans Hughes, Supreme Court justice and secretary of state.
421: Marshal Ferdinand Foch, World War I general.

East Hampton, L. I.

422

423

422: John Francis Hylan, mayor of New York 1918–25. 423: General Leonard Wood, army chief of staff 1910–14.

424

426

425

424: Joab H. Banton, Manhattan district attorney. 425: John W. Weeks, secretary of war under Harding. 426: John Purroy Mitchell, mayor of New York 1914–17.

427: James Wolcott Wadsworth, Jr., U.S. senator from New York. 428: Fiorello H. La Guardia (later mayor of New York) as a major in World War I. 429: President Calvin Coolidge. 430: William Jennings Bryan, lawyer and statesman.

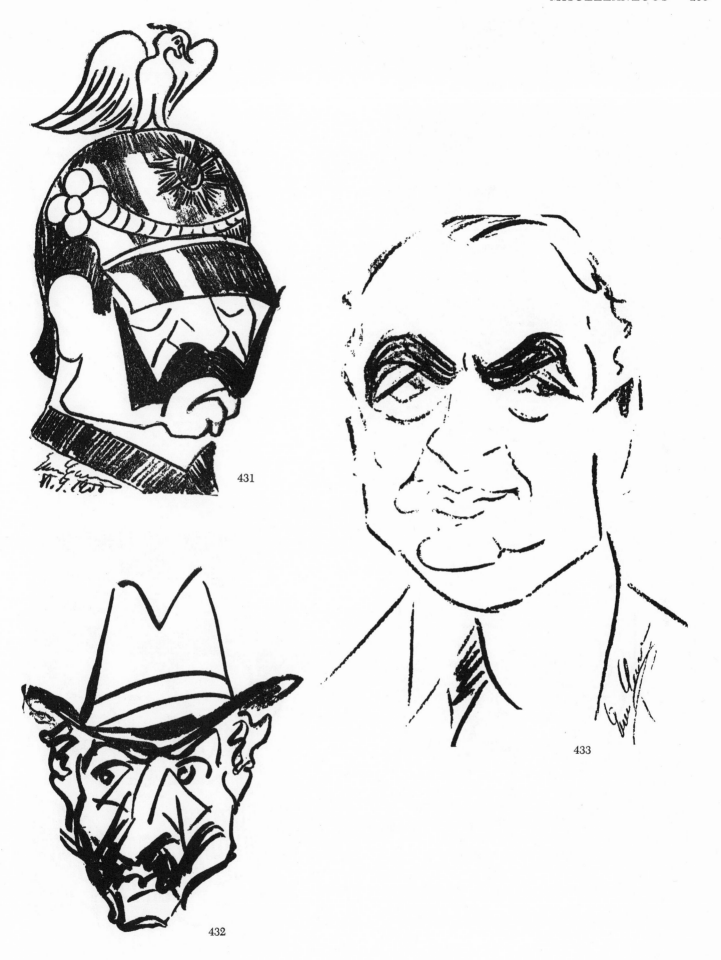

431 & 432: Kaiser Wilhelm II before and after abdication. 433: President Warren
G. Harding.

434: King Vittorio Emanuele III of Italy. 435: President Grover Cleveland.
436: Emperor Franz Josef of Austria. 437: President Theodore Roosevelt.

Per la "Follia" di N. Y.

439

438

438 & 439: King Alfonso XIII of Spain.

441

Sincerely
Enrico Caruso
N.Y. 1918

440

440 & 441: President Woodrow Wilson.

442: President William H. Taft. 443: Charles I, last emperor of Austria.
444: Bainbridge Colby, secretary of state under Wilson. 445: Berry Wall, socialite.

446: George V. Mullan, New York City judge. 447: Louis Wiley, journalist. 448: Sir Thomas Lipton, British tea magnate and yachtsman.

449

449: Guglielmo Marconi, inventor.

450: John Pierpont Morgan, financier. 451: John D. Rockefeller, oil czar.

452: William K. Vanderbilt, railroad executive. 453: General José Miguel Gómez, president of Cuba 1909–13. 454: General Álvaro Obregón, president of Mexico 1920–28.

455: King Ferdinand of Bulgaria. 456: Mario G. Menocal, president of Cuba 1913–21.
457: George B. McClellan, mayor of New York 1904–09.

458: Elihu Root, secretary of state under T. Roosevelt. 459: John Hay, secretary of state under McKinley and Roosevelt. 460: Luigi Amedeo, Duca degli Abruzzi, explorer and mountaineer.

461: Count István Tisza, premier of Hungary. 462: Theobald von Bethmann-Hollweg, chancellor of Germany 1909–17. 463: Enver Pasha, ruler of Turkey.

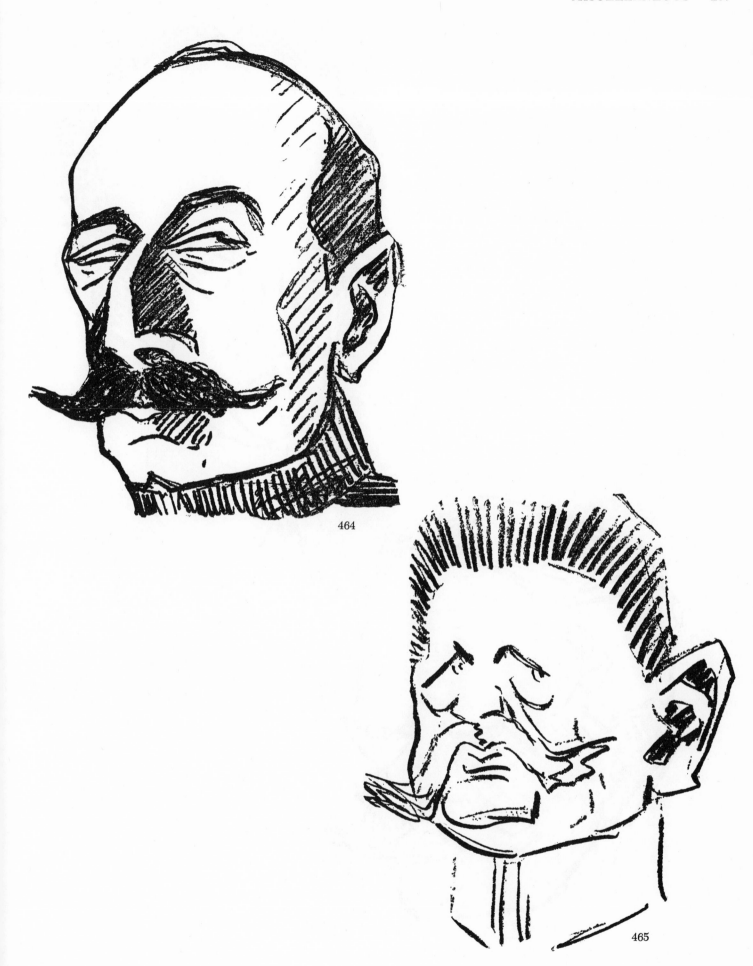

464: Prince Maximilian of Baden. 465: Paul von Hindenburg, German general (later president of Germany).

466: August von Mackensen, German general. 467: Count Johann Heinrich von Bernstorff, German ambassador to the U.S.

468

468: Unidentified (a tenor Gengardi or Genzardi?; reproduced from original drawing).

469

469: Unidentified (reproduced from original drawing).

470: Dr. Antonio Stella (reproduced from original drawing).

471

471: Unidentified (reproduced from original drawing).

472: Unidentified (reproduced from original drawing).

473

473: Joseph Bellanca (reproduced from original drawing).

INDEX

The numbers are those of the illustrations.